- Successful Dating -

No More Frogs
Virgo

23 August – 22 September

by
Cathrine Dahl

CONTENTS

- Successful Dating -
No More Frogs

by Cathrine Dahl

No More Frogs - Successful Dating is your one-stop dating guide. No unnecessary blah-blah. The information is right here, at your fingertips.

This guide can be used in several ways. It's a handy tool when you want to prepare yourself a little. It can give you an advantage when going on a date or getting to know someone you've just met - or even someone you've known for a while.

Although this guide can help you angle your approach, remember to be true to yourself. Have fun, be wise, follow your heart - and keep your feet on the ground!

- Cathrine Dahl

Preface:
A few words about compatibility, and why compatibility guides can give you the wrong idea.

So you've met this Gemini you really, really like, but you're a Scorpio, and the compatibility guides say you're a lousy match. Guess what? That's rubbish!

Some compatibility guides offer a very simplistic approach, claiming that your best matches are the star signs within the same element as you:

Fire: Aries, Leo and Sagittarius
Earth: Taurus, Virgo and Capricorn
Air: Gemini, Libra and Aquarius
Water: Cancer, Scorpio and Pisces

Other guides are slightly more specific, declaring that we are compatible with star signs within our astrological polarity.

Yin: Taurus, Virgo, Capricorn, Cancer, Scorpio and Pisces
Yang: Aries, Leo, Sagittarius, Gemini, Libra and Aquarius

Doesn't look too good, does it? The most optimistic approach has removed half of the population from your dating pool. It doesn't make any sense. The true picture is far more promising...

One star sign, two very different personalities

Each of us has a unique astrological thumbprint determined by the sun, the moon and the planets. The most important factors being your ascending star (ascendant), the sun (star sign) and the moon (feelings).

Let's make it simple
Imagine your star sign being a melody. All the other aspects (the unique positioning of the moon and the planets) are sound effects, applied by a producer with a mixer.

The combination of rhythm, depth and base creates your unique sound. Another person with the same star sign will get his own sound mix and end up with a different beat.

Your personal melody can create wonderful harmonies with star signs you're not supposed to get on with – and nothing but noise with signs that are meant to be matches. You won't find out until you get to know each other.

Let's get to know your date...

THE MALE

YOUR DATE: VIRGO
23 August – 22 September

The Essence of him

Intelligent – outgoing – charming – analytical – private – slightly split personality – strict perfectionist – thorough – down to earth – self-disciplined – workaholic – interesting – knowledgeable – health conscious – lone wolf – moody – temperamental – kind – assertive – polite – attentive – entertaining – helpful – loyal – considerate – practical – has a distinctive boyish nature, he'll never grow old

...and remember: Although he may come across as confident and outgoing, he can actually be a little shy when it comes to women. Go ahead and take the initiative, but be classy about it.

Blind Date – speedy essentials

Who's waiting for you?
He may try to be cool about it, but he'll be looking at his watch and towards the entrance. The anticipation can make him a little nervous, but don't be fooled, he's got everything under control. He has sorted out the dining options or whatever you've planned to do. He won't change his mind or pull out if he discovers that you're not his type. He'll see it through and make you feel comfortable in his company. This is a stylish guy. He's neat with a keen eye for detail – which means he'll be keeping an eye on your appearance too...!

Emergency fixes for embarrassing pauses
Although he usually drapes himself in self-confidence, he can get a little shy if you've managed to dazzle him with your sparkling laugh. Ask him about something and be smart about it. These guys usually know quite a bit about most things and they enjoy sharing the knowledge. If you manage to see everyday topics from new angles, then you won't have to worry about pauses.

Your place or mine?
Neither. If he's looking for a romantic relationship, he won't suggest having sex. An erotic invitation on the first date usually means he's more interested in your body than your mind and not a long term commitment. He's very patient. If he really likes you, he's prepared to get to know you and wait until he has met you two, three... or five, or seven times.

Checklist, before you dash out to meet him:

Hair in place, eyebrows fixed, well-kept hands
(hint: Be tidy)
Running on schedule
(hint: Don't be late)
Feeling good, no sniffles coming on
(hint: No germs)
Up to date on current affairs
(hint: Be alert)
Got some fun ideas and opinions
(hint: Be interesting)

Tip: NEVER hassle this guy. Fuss and high expectations can mess up work-relations and romantic feelings.

CHAPTER 1

PREPARE YOURSELF

Catch his eye, capture his attention
Top 10 attention grabbers

1. An alert mind and bright eyes.
2. Intelligent comments. Little sidekicks will make him pay attention.
3. Stylish and feminine clothing.
4. Sparkling playfulness - but no "dumb blonde".
5. Display a positive attitude towards others.
6. Ask for his opinion.
7. Display your sporty and healthy sides, but don't overdo it.
8. Emphasize the quality in you and everything you do.
9. Keep a positive outlook on life. Ease his mind if he seems stressed out.
10. Don't come on too strong. Make him feel relaxed in your company.

The SHE. The woman!

This man is extremely choosy. His dream date is intellectually alert – without threatening his professional authority. She is classy and good looking – without spending too much time in front of the mirror or wasting money on expensive creams, treatments and clothes. She is charming, sparkling and feminine – but never silly and giggling. Her outlook is down to earth, but still creative and independent. No wonder there are so many bachelors born under the sign of Virgo...

The Essence of her

Smart and intelligent – well informed and up to date on current affairs – tidy and well kept – independent – assertive without being pushy – feminine and classy – genuine – down to earth – interesting – not afraid of voicing her opinion or supporting unusual ideas – outgoing – disciplined – reliable and supportive – adaptable, without being easily led – organized – calm and collected when the world throws her a challenge

---

Virgo arousal meter

From 0 to 100... in several hours. This guy is not driven by intense passion. He's an explorer who takes it slow.

Remember: Be true to yourself

It doesn't matter if he is the most stunning guy you've ever met – if you don't match, you don't match. You may be able to put on a show for a while to hold his attention, but what's the point? We can't please everybody. We all have different needs, dreams, tastes and preferences. There's no such thing as a one-size-fits-all lover. Be yourself, and be true to who you are – always!

Very important: If you feel a cold coming on, call him and move the date to another day. DO NOT spend the evening sniffling around this guy!

CHAPTER 2

THE FIRST DATE

Getting your foot in the door
The basics

Be charming, stylish and almost a little dignified. Avoid anything that may give him the impression that you're easy.

Pay close attention to details. Apart from your outfit, make-up and hairstyle, your mind needs to be alert!

Humor is a big hit with these guys, but there's a difference between being humorous and being silly. Convey a bit of intelligence, you'll be scoring major points.

Inspire him. If you are good at something, let him know. If you can introduce him to a new interest, do so.

Show good taste. This does not only apply to food. It applies to everything! Quality matters very much for these people!

Look good. If he has invited you out, put on something feminine and elegant, and remember to show up on time.

Punctuality is very important when seducing this guy. He dislikes wasting time - and money - and having to wait will only put him in a bad mood.

Whatever you do...

• **DON'T** be late.

• **DON'T** look scruffy or wear too much makeup.

• **DON'T** ditch your manners.

• **DON'T** command the attention and interrupt him.

• **DON'T** sneeze and cough without be discreet about it.

Remember,
give him space and time to figure things out.

- **DON'T** make silly jokes on behalf of others.

- **DON'T** throw your money around.

- **DON'T** criticize people who work long hours.

- **DON'T** talk about illnesses you have had or may have.

- **DON'T** give the impression that you don't know much

about current affairs.

If you push him into making a decision, you may end up pushing him out of your life.

Signs you're in - or not

This can actually be a little tricky to determine. He is usually very charming and outgoing. However, that's no measure for his interest in you – at least not when it comes to romance. Never take anything for granted. A positive attitude may indicate that he finds you fun and interesting – as a friend.

The challenge with this guy is that he usually finds himself at a crossroad – friend, fun or lover. It may be difficult to interpret what goes on in his mind, but there are subtle signals which will indicate that you have sparked his fire:

Chances are he will...

- take the initiative to do something
- suggest getting together – privately
- splash out money on you
- suggest working out together
- ask for your opinion
- make you top priority, ahead of work and friends

Not your type? Making an exit

The Virgo has a very practical approach to these things. He doesn't waste his time on anything – or anyone. If things don't work out, he'll be off. Even though you feel you've made your best effort to come across as smart, intelligent and charming, this man is constantly analyzing you – without you even noticing. He'll be adding things together and creating his own perception of you, and he usually gets it spot on. If he thinks you won't be able to live up to his expectations, well, that's it for him. It's just a matter of finding his perfect mate – which isn't very easy...

However, there are slow movers. There are Virgos who may be too distracted by work or whatever to get the point. If his lack of spontaneity and joy is driving you nuts, if you're getting tired of his need for achievement, if you are craving romance and more passion in your life, you may need to push things in order for him to make a move.

Foolproof exit measures:

These suggestions may seem a little over the top, but if you're going to send him a message, you might as well do it thoroughly.

- Let yourself go. Skip waxing, manicures and hair appointments
- Criticize his analytical mind and accuse him of being hung up in details
- Blow all your money partying with friends
- Be late or forget about dates
- Talk about previous lovers and how good they were
- Make a mess in the kitchen, bathroom, living room... and leave it for him to tidy up

CHAPTER 3

SEX'N STUFF

Seductive moves:
How to get him in the mood:

Remember, you are dealing with a guy who'd rather flash his brain than his 'tool box'". Cheap hook-up lines and obvious seductive moves will do nothing but annoy him. This man regards sex as an aesthetic experience, and not a lesson in breath-taking gymnastics. In other words, be subtle.

Preferences and erotic nature

Many Virgos enjoy having sex in the shower. Apart from the fact that it feels good, it satisfies his need for cleanliness. Personal hygiene is important! An erotic suggestion when you return from the gym in your workout clothes is a no-no-no! However, let him sneak a peek while you're taking a shower, and he won't need much encouragement to take it from there.

He does have a liberal streak and is open to ideas, providing you don't go over the top. Introduce him to something new and suggest being a little more daring. Mr Virgo can be surprisingly passionate with the right encouragement. Although sex can be a great release for stress and bottled-up frustrations, make sure not to bother him when he's busy. Wait until he's ready for a 'time out'.

Hitting the right buttons

Although every sign has areas on the body that are more sensitive than others, individual sensitivity may vary quite a bit. Don't go body-blind. Honing in on these erogenous zones and forgetting the rest of him is not a good idea. Use these areas to create sparks while turning him on, and as a passion-booster when things get heated. Watch his body language – including the most obvious of signs. Open your mind to the sensuality of touch and taste.

Key areas
His midsection. Stomach and waist

Get it on
Don't poke around with his midsection unless you truly want to get intimate with him. His entire stomach area is particularly sensitive and usually brings out the passionate side of him (usually, because he is one of the most self-controlled guys in the zodiac.)

Arouse him
Your absolute best bet is to start working on his stomach area. Use very light touches when stroking him. He also loves having his tummy scratched with your fingernails – providing you do it carefully, of course. Don't forget to use your lips and tongue. Men born under this sign love the sensation of moist lips gently brushing his skin and a playful tongue running over the stomach. If the two of you are having a bath or a shower, make sure to caress his erogenous zone with soap and water.

Surprise him

Let's be realistic; this guy is far too disciplined to be easily surprised. Your best bet is to make it seem accidental. Allow him to sneak a peek at you when you're taking a shower. This is actually one of the things that can have a distracting – effect on him.

Spice it up

Play with taste and temperature. Apply a touch of ice cream to his tummy and gently enjoy it off him with your warm lips and tongue. Don't focus on just one spot. Use his entire midsection.

Remember: There are no shortcuts to his bed. He can't relax and focus on sex if he's got work on his mind, or if the apartment – or his partner – looks a mess.

His expectations

Communicate. You don't have to be a lioness in bed, you don't even have to be vocal, but make sure to express how you feel.

Be clear. Never leave him guessing.

All in, or out! This man never does things half way. If something is worth doing, it's worth doing well – an approach which applies to his erotic life as well.

Be vocal. He takes great pride in pleasing his woman and feedback is crucial. A quiet and non-expressive woman can make him feel insecure and turn him off completely.

Take the initiative. He doesn't mind a woman who takes the initiative in bed, providing she's playful and feminine.

No aggressiveness, please! Aggressive women turn him off, not only in bed but also in every other aspect of life.

Be creative. A creative partner can do wonders for his self-esteem. Sharing the responsibility while broadening his erotic horizons will make him relax and thoroughly enjoy the whole thing.

Guide him. Don't be afraid to guide him and drop a few hints. He'll appreciate it.

Your sensual preferences
Quiz yourself and find out whether this man is for you.

Where on the scale are you?
1 = Don't agree | 3 = Sure | 5 = Agree!

Question 1
Communication is important during sex
One a scale for 1 to 5, you are: 1 - 2 - 3- 4 - 5

Question 2
Creativity can make an erotic encounter more fulfilling
One a scale for 1 to 5, you are: 1 - 2 - 3- 4 - 5

Question 3
Playfulness can bring out passion and sensuality in you
One a scale for 1 to 5, you are: 1 - 2 - 3- 4 - 5

Question 4
Attention to personal hygiene is important before having sex
One a scale for 1 to 5, you are: 1 - 2 - 3- 4 - 5

Score 15–20: You share some of the essentials, which is a great base to build on.
Score 10–14: Your erotic differences can actually be an inspiration and make you grow.
Score 5–9: Never leave things to chance. Don't assume he knows what you want. Make sure your spontaneity doesn't make him feel obliged to perform.
Score 1–4: Make sure to communicate desires and expectations in order to avoid misunderstandings. An erotic chat before having sex could be a good idea.

CHAPTER 4

GENERAL STUFF

The big picture

Keep in mind that the characteristics of a Virgo may vary quite a bit depending on where within the sign he was born, as well as a wide range of additional astrological factors. But for now, let's stick to the basics. Just remember: don't jump to conclusions as soon as you meet him. Give him room to shine. Get to know the man behind the sign.

His personality: Pros and cons

Pros	Cons
• Focused	• Moody
• Kind and generous	• Temperamental
• Loyal and supportive	• Stressed
• Excellent sense of humour	• Workaholic
• Outgoing and charming	• Self-obsessed
• Reliable	• Pedantic perfectionist
• Boyish and active	• Split personality
• Intelligent	• Emotionally reserved
• Outgoing	• Overly health conscious
• Playful	• Wary of romantic commitment
• Knowledgeable	• Lone wolf
• Thorough	• Critical and analytical
• Eye for details	• Worrier
• Creative	• High expectations

Tip: How to show romantic interest

Appealing to his romantic nature is difficult. Romance is not his strongest side. Making an effort and doing something he doesn't expect you to do will always be interpreted positively.

Hint: Pay attention to his work and interests.

Romantic Vibes

Mr Virgo:
The supportive and inspirational partner

The essence

Reserved. He won't dazzle you with sweet nothings and declare his love for you. He's neither cold nor insensitive; he simply finds it a little difficult to talk about his feelings.

...but makes up for it. When he fails to express something with words, he makes up for it with actions.

Faithful. His partner doesn't have to worry about him running around. He takes commitment seriously.

Loyal. He will always show his woman great respect when out in public.

Romance. A relationship is far more than a romantic affair, it's a source of inspiration. He combines love and friendship and makes his partner his best friend.

Work. His partner must be prepared to compete with his work when days are hectic, but he will never abandon his woman for long – and he will always make it up to her.

Honesty. He is honest and direct in every aspect of his life. If he pays you a compliment, you can be sure he's being sincere.

Inspiring partner. It is very important that his partner is able to inspire him. If she doesn't, he'll get bored.

Tip: How to show erotic interest

Don't be obvious about it. Do and say things which might be interpreted in an erotic manner.

Play with your hair, caress yourself gently while reading or concentrating ...anything to make him pay attention – but make it seem casual.

Erotic Vibrations

Mr Virgo:
The cool and analytical lover

The essence

In control. Don't expect a fierce Latin lover to emerge as soon as the clothes are off. This guy is cool in bed as well.

Well prepared. He may ask you about your erotic preferences, simply because he wants everything to be right. Being prepared makes him relax.

Sensual sixth sense. He is a wonderful lover and seems to have a sixth sense when it comes to pleasing his partner.

Conservative - and funky. Although conservative and slightly traditional, he does have a liberal streak...

Erotic hors d'oeuvre. He is a master when it comes to foreplay, but may need a nudge if you don't want to spend hours before getting it on.

All-niter. Stamina is one of his strengths and he can keep going all night.

Open minded - kind of. He is open to suggestions, providing they are not vulgar.

The beauty of sensuality. This man regards sex as an aesthetic experience, not a lesson in breathtaking gymnastics.

CHAPTER 5

COMPATIBILITY QUIZ

Are you banging your head against the wall, or does he unleash your positive potential? Do you provoke him or bring out the best in him? Does he make you throw your arms up in exasperation, or do you feel inspired and complete in his company? Are the two of you headed towards doom or dream? Take the test to find out.

Question 1
What's your attitude to work and ambitions?

A. The sole purpose of a job is to make money.
B. If you want to achieve something in life, you need to make an effort.
C. It depends... I'd probably be more ambitious had my job been more interesting.

Question 2
Do you ever leave things to fate?

A. Never. People who rely on fate are seldom in control of their lives.
B. Sometimes, but only if I have no influence over the outcome of a situation.
C. Of course. Whatever happens, happens.

(cont.)

Question 3.
How do you react when a guy suggests taking a bath or a shower before having sex?

A. That's ok I guess. Never thought much about it.
B. Whenever I'm in a passionate mood, I don't want to run through the shower.
C. I don't mind. Foreplay in the shower can actually be very exciting.

Question 4.
Is it important that your partner clearly expresses his love for you?

A. Yes, I'm no mind reader.
B. My partner and I communicate very well. He only needs to look at me to convey how he feels about me.
C. Yes, but not necessarily with words. There are many other ways to show love and affection.

Question 5.
Would you describe yourself as a physically active person?

A. The only physical activity I'm into is sex.
B. I like hiking and going for walks. I find that very relaxing.
C. I enjoy a wide variety of sports, simply because I enjoy keeping active and staying in shape.

Question 6.
You've decided to seduce you partner one evening. How would you go about it?

A. Give him a sensual bath after a romantic dinner?
B. Depends on his mood, really.
C. Put on sassy underwear and stream a porn movie?

Question 7.
Do you tend to offer constructive criticism and firm advice?

A. Sometimes, but only if I feel it's needed.
B. Very seldom. Friendly hints and diplomacy usually produce better results.
C. Of course. I speak my mind. Honesty is important.

Question 8.
Do you think it's possible to have a rewarding relationship without making sex a major part of your lives?

A. Yes. Sensuality will develop naturally in any loving relationship.
B. No, sex is too important to be pushed aside.
C. I don't know. Erotic impulses make the days more exciting.

Question 9.
How do you feel about guys who suggest having sex on a first date?

A. Well, I'm quite passionate and if the atmosphere turns erotic then why not?
B. I'd be quite offended actually. I think that's cheap.
C. If everything was right. If it was love at first sight. If there's such a thing as dream partner. Until then, I'd probably turn him down.

Question 10.
Do you tend to get easily stressed?

A. Not stressed, but engaged and active. Adrenaline keeps me going.
B. Not really, I'm quite grounded and manage to see things for what they are.
C. Yes, and I tend to worry about things.

SCORE	A	B	C
Question 1	1	10	5
Question 2	10	5	1
Question 3	5	1	10
Question 4	1	10	5
Question 5	1	5	10
Question 6	10	5	1
Question 7	5	10	1
Question 8	10	1	5
Question 9	1	10	5
Question 10	5	10	1

75 – 100

You've finally found the man who brings balance and harmony into your life. You respect his ideals and admire his self-discipline. He makes you feel proud when you're out with friends. You love the way he pampers you and protects you. His unique ability to bring out the best in you, makes you shine. He expects you to be independent and capable of taking care of yourself, but he will always be by your side whenever you need encouragement and a helping hand. A relationship like this will become stronger as time goes by and allow both of you to keep growing. This is a perfect match.

51 – 74

Romantic love and friendship is a perfect combination. This man will give you space as well as treating you to lots of intimacy. He will broaden your horizon with his amazing knowledge - and make you feel like a princess in bed. Life is never boring with Mr. Virgo around. He may get obsessive about detail from time to time, but that's a small price to pay considering all the wonderful things he brings in to your life. He may dish out a few truths from time to time, and give you a verbal kick in the backside if he feels you're getting a tad lazy, but he usually prefers to inspire. When he commits himself to you, you won't have to doubt his love and affection.

26 – 50

This relationship may be a challenge at times, but life is filled with challenges which makes us stronger. Sometimes the two of you seem to be heading off in different directions, which may cause a few discussions. His practical approach may drive you slightly nuts and make you long for a bit more passion in your life. Despite all this, there's something that makes you stay by his side. He is a rare, no-nonsense-guy who makes you feel safe. However, you may reach a point where you need decide. If you keep suppressing your need for excitement and adventure, it will only make you miserable. Life with Mr. Virgo can be hard work, but it can also be very loving and rewarding. In the end it will be a matter of values and what it takes to make both of you happy. Think about it, the choice is yours.

10 – 25

Have you given in to conformity? Have you become a creature of habit, accepting Mr. Virgo's firm suggestions? Are you fascinated by his nice and trim body - which he works out in the gym and not in bed? Are you getting used to playing second fiddle and pushing your own needs and dreams aside? Wake up. Do a reality check and listen to your heart. Be honest with yourself, is there a lot of romance and passion in your life? What are you longing for? Don't waste your life on a partner who's not satisfying your basic needs. He may be nice and kind, but is it worth it? A more suitable partner may be waiting for you elsewhere.

Thoughts...

Love conquers everything, including compatibility guides, partner quizzes and astrological do's and don'ts.

If the man makes you happy, no matter how challenging it might be, give him a chance, give it a try. Just remember, be true to yourself.

THE FEMALE

YOUR DATE: VIRGO
23 August – 22 September

The Essence of her

Naturally charming – choosy – high expectations – loyal to her friends and family – thorough and detailed – modest – supportive – independent – sensible and down to earth – attractive – determined – feminine and sparkling – tends to worry about details – practical – analytical – childish curiosity – sets high standards for herself and people around her – health conscious – strict work ethics

...and remember: She may strike you as strong and independent, but the essence of her has a modest streak. Deep down she is looking for a man who can protect her and keep her safe.

Blind Date – speedy essentials

Who's waiting for you?

She should NOT be waiting for you. You must be there when she arrives. The fact that you've managed to get her to go on a blind date with you, is a quite a feat. Don't mess it up by being late. This is a real woman, something you'll notice right away. She is charming, feminine and slightly reserved. But there is something about her you cannot figure out... She seems independent and strong, but at the same time modest and sensitive. That's the essence of her. She can handle world by herself, but she'd rather have a man by her side to help and protect her. But she's choosy...

Emergency fixes for embarrassing pauses.

Don't despair if the conversation slows down a little. She has a modest streak and can get a little sky. Gently guide the conversation onto something positive and safe – avoid the latest stupidity from the political scene. Show interest in her and what she's doing, without being inquisitive. Make her feel relaxed in your company.

Your place or mine?

Neither. Sex on a first date is not an option. For her to let go of her inhibitions and give in to erotic feelings, she needs to feel completely relaxed. To be relaxed with someone she doesn't know – on a first date – is not easy. You may charm her, but that doesn't mean she is sexually attracted to you. In her opinion, dropping the clothes on a first date is a bit tacky and her style.

Checklist, before you dash out to meet her:

Clean shirt, polished shoes, nice haircut
(hint: Be tidy)
No heavy cologne or other smells
(hint: Her tolerance is low)
Cell phone on silent
(hint: Focus on her)
Hungry, but not starving
(hint: Enjoy your food, slowly)
Up to date on interesting topics
(hint: Appeal to her mind)

Tip: You cannot fake your way to her heart or bed. She won't let you into her life before she knows and trusts you. A fling with her is not very likely.

CHAPTER 1

PREPARE YOURSELF

Catch her eye, capture her attention
Top 10 attention grabbers

1. Be stylish, masculine and polite.
2. Warm voice and gentle eyes.
3. Be completely focused on her. Forget the other women in the room.
4. In a restaurant, know your stuff (food and wine), but don't be a show-off.
5. Show consideration for others. Let her know you have a big heart.
6. Pay attention to your hands... make sure they look good.
7. Make the conversation relaxed and entertaining.
8. Keep it humorous and make her laugh.
9. Pay attention to details and behave like a gentleman.
10. Be generous without splashing money around.

The HE. The man!

Her dream partner doesn't fuss about sex, he doesn't interrupt her when she's busy – and he knows there is a time and place for everything. He's also very practical and able to fix things. A dreamy poet who's unable to change a light bulb, is not her kind of man. If he's smart, ambitious and good in the kitchen – and leaves it spotless after cooking – she will start paying attention...

The Essence of him

Practical – fit and healthy – down to earth – manly, without being overly masculine – organized in all areas of life – generous, without wasting his money – creative and able to introduce her to new adventures in life – reliable, and provides her with security – stylish with a sense of quality – interesting and intelligent – good sense of humour – positive outlook on life.

Virgo arousal meter
From 0 to 100... In an hour – if she knows you and feels comfortable around you. The passion needs to build gradually.

Remember: Be true to yourself

It doesn't matter if she is the most stunning girl you've ever met – if you don't match, you don't match. You may be able to put on a show for a while to hold her attention, but what's the point? We can't please everybody. We all have different needs, dreams, tastes and preferences. There's no such thing as a one-size-fits-all lover. Be yourself, and be true to who you are – always!

Very important: Be attentive to detail. Make sure your appearance is spotless, your manners are flawless and the evening is priceless – without spending too much money.

CHAPTER 2

THE FIRST DATE

Getting your foot in the door
The basics

Measure up. There is no such thing as an easy access to this woman's heart or bed. In order to win her you need to measure up to her standards and expectations.

Appeal to her mind. In order to succeed, you need to appeal to her intellect. Her head, not her feelings, rule her heart.

Be worth while, fun, be interesting. A smart guy with a sense of humour gets her attention.

Be strong. Being able to convey strength is a good thing. Deep down she wants a man who can protect her. Her ideal man makes her relax and stop worrying. He will tell her "Don't worry, it will be all right" - and make her believe it.

Make it classy. Invite her out, but not to a noisy restaurant. She prefers intimacy. Try a quiet and romantic little bistro.

No free spending. Don't waste your money on an expensive meal. She hates to see people throw money around.

Be patient. Never rush her into making a decision.

Whatever you do...

- **DON'T** show up in a dirty shirt. She spots a spot easily.

- **DON'T** drink too much or fork down your food.

- **DON'T** be loud and tell silly jokes.

- **DON'T** be late – never keep her waiting.

- **DON'T** throw your money around to impress her.

Remember,
show interest but take it slow.
Be persistent without being
pushy.

- **DON'T** rush her into making a decision.

- **DON'T** come on too strong.

- **DON'T** expect her to be erotically interested in you

right away.

- **DON'T** forget your manners. She will notice…

- **DON'T** bring up sex and erotic topics.

Be stylish without being flashy. Be masculine without being macho. Be genuine.

Signs you're in - or not

It can be a little tricky to figure out if you have managed to do more than just spark her interest. Even though she may feel quite enthusiastic about you, she will seldom show it right away. She needs to digest the impulses and think about it. She never hurries these things, but she won't delay it either. She is practical and aware that if she doesn't make a move, some other woman will. Keep in mind she has a modest streak, which can make it a little difficult to interpret her hints. However, there are signs she is eager to spend more time with you:

Chances are she will...

- text or call you back right away
- ask you to help her with something
- ask for your opinion
- mention an activity or an event, and make subtle hints...
- offer to help you with a practical task (organizing etc)
- take time off to see you and introduce you to her friends

Not your type? Making an exit

The Virgo female doesn't move from one relationship to the other, nor give in to love easily. When she has finally found someone she is willing to commit to, she will strive hard to make things work. Although she gets emotionally attached to her partner, her life is run by reason. She would rather spend life on her own than in a destructive relationship. She does snap when her partner is not living up to her standards, but mostly because she wants to help him.

Leaving her could be easy, or it could be a little tricky. It all depends on how long you've been together. The older the relationship, the more difficult it gets. 'Forgive and forget' becomes easier as time goes by – providing you're not driving her nuts and she's about to say ENOUGH! However, if she holds on to you and her vision of love, you may want to be blunt about it.

Foolproof exit measures:

Although she is calm and down to earth, she does get hurt and upset. You need be absolutely sure before moving on with these measures.

- Make a mess, everywhere. Stop cleaning up after you
- Skip the laundry. Put on dirty shirts and sweaters
- Waste money. Tell her you're thinking about taking up gambling
- Insist on having sex all hours of the day, especially when she's busy
- Start complaining about politics, the weather, the lot
- Never be on time for dates or dinners

CHAPTER 3

SEX'N STUFF

Seductive moves:
How to get her in the mood:

The inner voice keeps messing things up. She really wants to let her hair down, but the good girl says no. That's why you may experience her eyes saying yes, but her voice saying no. A little confusing, but with the right encouragement you can make her feel naughty – and feel good about it.

Preferences and erotic nature

This may sound a little weird, but she's actually turned on by a man who knows how to fix things and handle domestic housework. Being good in the kitchen is a great plus. A sexy guy doing housework triggers her far more than other women in the zodiac.

A sudden funny and erotic comment can take her by surprise and make her think. If she's in the right mood, this will act as a self-starter. As soon as you have got her going, she will probably start smiling mischievously. She may give the impression of being proper, but with the right encouragement, you'll discover she's got a dirty mind...

Hitting the right buttons

Although every sign has areas on the body that are more sensitive than others, individual sensitivity may vary quite a bit. Don't go body-blind. Honing in on these erogenous zones and forgetting the rest of her is not a good idea. Use these areas to create sparks while turning her on, and as a passion-booster when things get heated. Watch her body language – including the most obvious of signs. Open your mind to the sensuality of touch and taste.

Key areas
Her stomach and waist

Get it on
Never make funny remarks about her tummy because this is one of her most sensitive areas - both mentally and physically. You can provoke all sorts of reactions by touching her stomach. Remember, and this is very important: NEVER touch her in such a way that she may think you're implying she has gained weight.

Arouse her
Be playful and seductive and you won't have to wait long for a positive reaction. It is very important that your touches are gentle and delicate, otherwise you risk turning her off. Suggest taking a shower or bath together. This will give you lots of opportunities to play with her erogenous zone. A casual massage is another option. Start with the back, and finish with the tummy. If you do it right, this could move on to something more sensual.

Surprise her

She's not really into surprises when it comes to sex, but a nice setting can get her going – providing she's not busy. Soft music, candles, warm oil and tasty snacks can make her relax and tune into your mood...

Spice it up

Try to experiment with oils, creams and perhaps even honey. Keep in mind, she can be a little inhibited at first, so take it slow.

Remember: She doesn't have an erotic on-button. She needs to be tuned in and turned up – not turned on. This requires patience, but it's worth it.

Her expectations

Make it sensual. She prefers lovemaking to be calm, close and sensual - with no passionate outbursts!

Make it comfortable. A dimly lit bedroom makes her feel comfortable. Forget about mirrors. This will only make her feel self-conscious and ruin the mood.

A little romance is fine... She will never overdo anything. A candle and a bottle of wine by the bedside is more than enough.

Turn on the shower... She enjoys foreplay in the bathroom. She loves the sensation of your wet body rubbing against hers. Besides, it's nice to freshen up a little before having sex... Don't take it the wrong way, just enjoy her sensual hands gently caressing you with a soft, foaming soap all over.

No acrobatics, please. In bed, she feels comfortable with the traditional positions. However, if you have something different in mind, tell her. She will probably try it - providing it it's not vulgar. If you really want to make her happy, be gentle!

Your sensual preferences
Quiz yourself and find out whether this woman is for you.

Where on the scale are you?
1 = Don't agree | 3 = Sure | 5 = Agree!

Question 1
Casual sex is too superficial to give any real enjoyment.
One a scale for 1 to 5, you are: 1 - 2 - 3- 4 - 5

Question 2
Comfortable surroundings and a nice setting is important.
One a scale for 1 to 5, you are: 1 - 2 - 3- 4 - 5

Question 3
Having sex when your mind is busy is not a good idea.
One a scale for 1 to 5, you are: 1 - 2 - 3- 4 - 5

Question 4
Taking a bath or a shower together can be very sensual.
One a scale for 1 to 5, you are: 1 - 2 - 3- 4 - 5

Score.
15 - 20: You are very much on the same level and able to read each other's signals. This will create harmony and sensuality.
10 - 14: You may be able to inspire each other and broaden the erotic horizon.
05 - 09: Hinting may not be enough. Make sure to be direct in order to avoid misunderstandings.
01 - 04: This could be a challenge, or it could be a step in to a new erotic world. It depends very much on flexibility and erotic interest.

CHAPTER 4

GENERAL STUFF

The big picture

Keep in mind that the characteristics of a Virgo may vary quite a bit depending on where within the sign she was born, as well as a wide range of additional astrological factors. But for now, let's stick to the basics. Just remember: don't jump to conclusions as soon as you meet her. Give her room to shine. Get to know the woman behind the sign.

Her personality: Pros and cons

Pros
- Natural charm
- Loyal
- Dependable
- Thorough
- Stylish and feminine
- Intelligent
- Genuine and honest
- Determined
- Compassionate
- Good sense of humour
- Down to earth
- Supportive
- Sensible

Cons
- Critical
- Uptight
- Picky
- Good girl/sacrifices herself
- Worries
- Fixed opinions
- Modest
- Stuck in her ways
- Overly health conscious
- Hung up on details
- Rigid in her ways
- High expectations of others
- Perfectionist

Tip: How to show romantic interest

Offer to help her with practical tasks.

Although independent and capable, she enjoys a man who can fix things. It makes her feel safe and protected. Afterwards, cook her something or invite her out.

Romantic Vibes

Miss Virgo:
The warm and supportive partner

The essence

Determined. She knows what she wants. This can be a blessing – and it can be a curse. In her quest for the perfect man, she follows her mind and not her heart. This may cause her to miss out on life's romantic opportunities. If she manages to let go of her romantic checklist, new opportunities will brighten her day.

Thinks twice... She's not easily carried away by romantic feelings and she will always think twice before giving in to love.

Realistic. Living on love alone is not her thing. Love may lose its sparkle, when reality sets in. However, life without love is grey and meaningless. She's a romantic in disguise.

Loving and genuine. She is affectionate and supportive. Honesty means a lot to her and an open dialogue is very important.

Strength and masculinity. Although she's very independent and strong, she needs a partner who makes her feel safe and cared for.

Affectionate. She seldom expresses feelings with words, but she will always make sure he knows how she feels about him.

Tip: How to show erotic interest

Don't be obvious about it. A gentle –
and seemingly casual – massage can
be a good place to start. Make sure to
choose the right time, and take it slow.

Erotic Vibrations

Miss Virgo:
The cool and controlled lover

The essence

No-nonsense attitude. She sometimes asks herself: What's the big deal? She has a practical attitude to sex.

Closeness and tenderness. She prefers gentleness and closeness, and the comfort of traditional lovemaking.

Ease into it. It's important to take it slow and tune her into sex. A man who throws himself at her will simply crush her. Arousing her takes gentle patience and a touch of finesse.

No flings. She very seldom has sex with someone she meets at a party or on a first date. She needs to know him – at least a bit – and feel comfortable around him.

An amazing lover. When she finally decides to unbutton, she won't disappoint. She is feminine, gentle and loving.

No worries, no pressure. She's very understanding. Should her partner fail to get his toolbox sorted out, she will patiently arouse him until he is ready to go.

Comfort. The setting is very important. It doesn't have to be over the top, just pleasant and comfortable.

Keep it genuine. Sex should be natural and filled with joy. She will never turn sex into physical exercise.

CHAPTER 5

COMPATIBILITY QUIZ

Are you banging your head against the wall, or does she unleash your positive potential? Do you provoke her or bring out the best in her? Is she making you throw your arms into the air in exasperation, or do you feel inspired and complete in her company? Take the test to find out.

Question 1
Do you expect to go to bed with a woman on a first date?

A - Of course. When I go on a blind date, I want some fun.
B – Depends on the woman.
C - No! That's not my style. I prefer to get to know a woman before going to bed with her.

Question 2
Is a passionate partner important to you?

A - No. I believe closeness, mutual respect and intimate sex are much more important.
B - Passion is important, but not it's the most important thing.
C - Sex without passion is not sex, it's housewife aerobics.

(cont.)

Question 3.
How do you respond when your girlfriend suggests having a bath before making love?

A - That's OK I guess, I've never really thought about it. It could be fun.
B - How boring. When I'm ready for sex, I want sex not a bath!
C – Love the sensation of wet bodies against each other.

Question 4.
What do you regard as most important when entering an erotic relationship?

A - Sensuality and sensuality only.
B - Passion.
C - Compatibility - and erotic chemistry, of course.

Question 5.
You have decided to seduce you partner one evening. What do you do?

A - Stream a porn movie.
B – Make sure the setting is right... candles, soft music... the lot.
C - Buy her a bunch of flowers - and some sexy underwear.

Question 6.
Do you always expect your partner to show her feelings?

A - No. Sometimes it's better to handle your own issues without the interference from others.
B - That depends very much on the situation.
C - Of course I do. How else am I supposed to know what's on her mind?

Question 7.
Do you enjoy lots of foreplay?

A - Well, I guess that can be okay. I haven't really thought about that.
B - Yes. Foreplay makes the orgasm much more intense.
C – No. Too much foreplay makes me sleepy.

Question 8.
How do you feel about a cool and reserved woman?

A – It depends very much on the input I get – but I like a bit of mystery.
B – I avoid women like that. They annoy me.
C - Hmmm... There are many sides to a woman. A cool woman may be hiding some sparkling and hot sides to her personality....

Question 9.
Do you expect your girlfriend to take the initiative to sex?

A - Not really. Whenever we have sex it just happens.
B - Why am I supposed to take the initiative all the time?
C - I don't expect her to do so - but it's always nice when she does...

Question 10.
Have you ever caressed you partner without using your hands?

A - Without using my hands? Am I missing something here?
B - Yes, several times. It's really nice, especially when we are covered in oil...
C – Yes, when we share closeness through hugging.

SCORE	A	B	C
Question 1	1	5	10
Question 2	10	5	1
Question 3	5	1	10
Question 4	5	1	10
Question 5	1	10	5
Question 6	10	5	1
Question 7	1	10	5
Question 8	5	1	10
Question 9	10	1	5
Question 10	1	10	5

75 – 100

You have managed to find a great balance between work, sensuality and every day creativity. Even though your erotic life may not be described as hot and steamy, it's very intense and fulfilling. Sex is no big deal, as such. It's an important spice in your life, but not a hobby. This is what makes this relationship so special. Everything seems to be balanced. No matter how busy it gets, you always manage to find time for each other – to enjoy and inspire. You are on the same level and communicate with ease and love. Enjoy!

51 – 74

What have you done to her? Have you noticed the sparkle in her eyes? The enthusiasm and the happiness that surrounds her? It's called bringing out the best in people, and that's what you've managed to do. It feels so good to be on the same level with someone. To feel safe, to feel loved - to feel desired. Everything is running so smoothly. Just remember not rush her. You don't want to risk losing this unique opportunity. Sensual feelings are easily brought to life in the bathroom. Why not ask her to rub your back while taking a shower or a bath and let things develop from there... She is far more passionate than people think – and you know that.

26 – 50

If you don't share the same values. If you don't see eye to eye on the most basic questions, there will be discussions – quite a few discussions. You won't be able to move forward unless you find something that unites you, something fundamental that binds you together. Right now, you're more eager to prove you're right and try to convince the other, rather than working together. Open your mind and try to see things from different angles. Forget about right or wrong – expand your vision and your horizons. Love is a strong force. If you really feel strongly about it, bring it out and see what happens. You either move forward together or continue separately.

10 – 25

Things could probably be a lot better. Why are you sticking with her? Because she keeps your life nice and organized? How about your sex life? Not so good? Well, if sex ranks on top of your list of priorities, you're probably better off somewhere else. The two of you are so different. How you managed to get together in the first place is a great mystery. Your values are different. Your goals are different. Your needs are different... Love conquers all, but is it really love you're feeling? Maybe it's time to move on. Happiness awaits elsewhere – for both of you.

Thoughts…

It's not the score in this quiz which determines whether you will score with her. Maybe you are the jigsaw piece she is missing to make her picture complete.

Happiness is precious. If you have found happiness with her, cherish it!

...just a final note:
This book has not been approved by your date and should be treated accordingly. He or she *may* not agree with the content.

www.ingramcontent.com/pod-product-compliance
Lightning Source LLC
Chambersburg PA
CBHW071839020426
42331CB00007B/1787